MW00674376

CAREERS IN INFORMATION TECHNOLOGY

By
MELANIE ANN APEL

The Rosen Publishing Group, Inc.
New York

Published in 2000 by The Rosen Publishing Group, Inc.
29 East 21st Street, New York, NY 10010

Copyright © 2000 by Melanie Ann Apel

First Edition

Library of Congress Cataloging-in-Publication Data

Apel, Melanie Ann.
    Careers in information technology / by Melanie Ann Apel.
      p.   cm.
    Includes bibliographical references and index.
    Summary: Examines the careers available in the fields of information management, computers, the Internet, and software development, discussing the necessary education and training.
    ISBN 0-8239-2892-6
    1. Computer science—Vocational guidance—Juvenile literature.
2. Information technology—Vocational guidance—Juvenile literature.
[1. Computer science—Vocational guidance. 2. Information technology—Vocational guidance. 3. Vocational guidance.] I. Title.
    QA76.25 .A64 2000
    004'.023—dc21   00-028592

Manufactured in the United States of America

About the Author

Melanie Ann Apel has a bachelor's degree in respiratory care and another in theater arts. She has written a number of children's books on health-related topics. She lives in Chicago, Illinois.

Acknowledgments

Without the wealth of knowledge (and a great deal of patience) provided to me so lovingly by Denise Pagel Moskovitz and Wade Brown, and the hands-on assistance of Mindy Apel, this book would not have come to be. With love right back to you: Thank you.

I also wish to thank the following people who answered my questions and generously shared the details of their careers with me: Matt Helms, Samantha Hoffman, John Hutton, Michael Jaltuch, Ed Kuehl, Jay Leib, Barbara Radomsky, Michael Radomsky, Nagesh Reddy, Adam Frederickson, and Julia James. And to those who continue to offer the greatest measures of support and encouragement: Carol and Darwin Apel, Michele Hammer Ottenfeld, Lisa Radek Tolnai, and Jennifer Logothetti Gordon—thank you, too.

Contents

Introduction

Information technology? Have you ever heard a defini-
tion of information technology? Considering that you
have picked up this book, there is a good chance that
you have already heard the term. But what is information technology, you ask? Believe it or not, it is
exactly what it sounds like. Information technology is
a career field in which people take information in one
form and "process" it, that is, convert it into another
form that other people can use more easily. The
actual term "information technology" encompasses a
very broad field, and its meaning actually varies
depending on the field you are in. In its most general
meaning, information technology means maintaining
and accessing information. However, this accessing
and maintenance of information can be done in different ways, depending on whether you are working
on the Internet, in a book-based library, in a research
lab, or for a general business.

Information technology is all around us. These
days, information technology most often involves the
use of computers. However, there are still many older
types of information technology that are still in use
today that do not involve computers at all. So, in the
broadest sense, information technology can be
described as the study of the process of maintaining
and distributing information, especially (but not
exclusively) in an electronic form.

Common examples of information technology in current use range from the most basic forms, using paper and pencil to transmit information, to large, complex forms involving high-tech computer-based systems. A couple of other commonly used terms that are basically interchangeable with information technology are "information systems" and "information science." Occasionally you will hear the term "data warehousing." All these terms basically mean the same thing. To quote Chicago-based Web administrator Denise Pagel, "The term 'systems' is more likely to be used by a person trained in computers. The term 'science' is more of a term commonly used by librarians. However, for purposes here, a sofa is the same as a couch." For the purposes of this book, all three terms—information science, information systems, and information technology—will be used to mean the same thing.

But what does all this mean? How does this affect you and your future? Is information technology a field you would like to explore further and perhaps make a career of? This book will take you on a journey through the world of information technology. It will introduce and discuss various jobs within the field, lay out the requirements for someone who wants to enter the field, and help you determine whether or not this is a good field for you to join through a series of self-examination questions. By the time you have finished reading this book in its entirety, you will have learned something about how to get started in the field of information technology, including what classes you should be taking in high school and what to expect when you finally land a job in the field. You will have an idea of the range of salaries for different positions in the field. You will be equipped with a list of resources, including books to read, Web sites to visit, colleges to consider and what they require from incoming freshmen, periodicals you can subscribe to, and professional organizations from which you can gather further information. You will have some idea as to what the future of information technology holds, as well as a little bit of the history of computers and information systems. You will also have the distinct privilege of taking an intimate peek at the career paths of some real professionals employed in some of the various areas of the industry. These people will describe how they got into their particular fields, what they believe you should study in high school in order to prepare to work in the field, and how they have moved up within their profession. They will discuss the strengths they possess that helped them get where they are, their general opinions of the field as a whole, and the roles they play in the field of information technology every day.

As I work to finish writing this book, pulling scraps of paper with notes scratched on the back of them from my coat pockets, and then sitting at my computer to type it all in, I am struck by the irony of my situation. Conducting research for this book has been in and of itself an exercise in utilizing the networks of information technology. The majority of the material in this book was gathered while sitting right here at my desk, via my computer. I searched the Internet for Web sites containing information about information technology. I had conversations and conducted interviews with information technology professionals via e-mail. In fact, all of the professionals who provided me with information did so via e-mail except for two, whose information came via an older information system: the telephone. It really does go to show you that computers and information technology really do touch just about everyone in almost every aspect of work and home life. Things just would not be the same if it were not for the advances in technology that bring us the elaborate network of people, machines, and data that we refer to collectively as information technology.

1

What Is Information Technology?

You may have just picked this book up off the bookshelf without knowing anything at all about information technology. However, it is more likely that you have some idea about the field and what it entails, and that you picked up this book for a particular reason. What you are probably looking for is more information. Perhaps you even want enough information to help you decide whether or not a career in information technology is for you. You are in luck. This book is just what you need.

Since the middle of the last century, that is, about fifty years ago, computers have virtually taken over the world as we know it, especially in the areas of information and communications. The work people do today is far different from the work done by your parents and grandparents. Sure, the outcome of the tasks may be fundamentally the same, but the paths you take to obtain your information and get things done are greatly different and far more efficient today than the methods used in generations past. The effects of the computer and the information it makes available are felt by people all over the world. From the student sitting at his or her desk at home looking up information to write a paper, to the large corporation comparing this year's sales to last year's sales for all of its worldwide branches, the computer has made its mark everywhere. Computers are used in just about every field, opening up thousands of career opportunities for people who have computer literacy and professional experience. As you have probably realized, all of these jobs are relatively new. None of them existed in the day when your grandparents were going to work!

WELCOME

Welcome to the exciting world of information technology, where the mere stroke of your finger across a keyboard can instantly transport you to a vast world of information. And what's more, the possibility exists for you to make this fascinating world your career. People seek and gather information for both the purposes of work and for leisure. Click your mouse on a Web site. Access facts and data to write your term paper. Look up stock quotes. Collect statistics about how much money you could make working in the field of information technology. Find out which states are the best to travel to during the summer. Look up the movies playing at your neighborhood movie theater. The possibilities of available information are endless. It is all there, all at the click of your mouse. And the best part is, there are careers that center on preparing, setting up, gathering, accessing, and using this wealth of information.

As you head into adulthood, you may not yet know for sure what you want to do with your life. Even if you are only just contemplating information technology as your career, you do already know one important thing. You want to be successful in what you do. The key to success, as you may already have guessed, is information. Whether you are using the information as a tool to further your career or you are already working within an information field, the necessity for information—easily accessible and in large quantities—is tangible.

You are about to learn just how integral information, computers, and the networks that connect the two are to one another. What an exciting, up-and-coming career field! Information and success, they go hand in hand, and if you choose to pursue a career in information technology, both will be in your hands!

Information technology is a set of "systems used to transport information and make that information available where it will do some good," says California-based Web master Wade Brown. The field is broad and actually encompasses many different types of jobs. Most of these jobs have something to do with working with computers. Take a look at the following list of jobs that are considered part of the field of information technology:

- Communications
- Computer Design
- Computer Manufacturing
- Computer Programming
- Computer Sales
- Computer Service
- Database Management
- Data Service Organizations
- Expert Systems
- Information Science Management
- Internet
- Intranet
- Networks
- Operations
- Personal Computers
- Personal Computer User Services
- Security
- Systems Analysis

- Systems Development and Programming
- Word Processing

Do any of these fields sound at all familiar to you? Perhaps you know someone who works in one or more of these fields. Please note that quite often two or more of these jobs will overlap in a person's job description.

Information technology is a very important part of all major (and quite a few minor) businesses and organizations in today's society. In fact, information technology may even play a large role in your everyday life. Do you own a computer? Do you use it to communicate with other people, to gather information, to learn, or to share information? If you do even one of these things with your computer, you are already using information technology. If this is interesting to you, perhaps you really would like to join the millions of people who make professional careers out of their interest in computers and information technology. Information professionals work in practically every industry you can imagine. Why? The answer is simple. Because computers are everywhere. They are newer and better all the time, and someone needs to keep up with that growth. Computers and computer technology are responsible for the fantastic special effects you see when you go to see movies like *Titanic* and *Star Wars*. Computers are also responsible for such fun things as computer games. In fact, throughout the entertainment industry, computers play a large role, bringing us the best in music, film, and art.

The field of crime fighting is another important area in which computers and databases have been used for several years now. In fact, computers and databases have become an extraordinarily important set of tools in the field of crime fighting. Databases were set up several years ago to help the police track everything from stolen cars to missing children to criminals. Just a few years ago, the Missing Children Act was passed into law to protect the interest of the countless numbers of children reported missing across the country every year. The act set up a centralized database of missing children to aid in the search for them and their rescue. The database helps law enforcement officers on both the local and state levels to search for, locate, and identify children who are missing because they were abducted or they ran away. Thanks to this innovative database, authorities are able to locate and identify many of the two million children who are reported missing every year. The act put another database into place as well. This database tracks the unidentified bodies of some of the missing children who turn up dead. It is sad that such a database is needed, but it has saved many families from emptying out their entire savings accounts to continue to search for a child who is dead but not yet identified.

INFORMATION TECHNOLOGY AND COMPUTERS

You may think that we have just strayed from the field of information technology and moved onto the field of computers. We have not. This just illustrates the close link between the two. Once again, a reminder: Information technology transports information and makes it available where it can do some good. So, let us continue. What other computer uses can you think of? In the world of sports, computers are used to give instant information on what each team is doing. People can actually watch a game on television while also tracking the plays on a computer at the same

9

time. Bankers use computers to keep track of the money that is coming in and going out of their banks. Perhaps you have gone to several branches of your own bank. You may have noticed that all the branches of your bank have complete information about your account, regardless of where you opened the account. The library works this way, as well, which you might have noticed if you have ever needed to borrow a book by interlibrary loan, in which your library finds the book you need from another library. One library taps into the database of other libraries to find the book you are looking for.

Networks, which you will learn more about shortly, are the paths by which personal computers (PCs), minicomputers, and large mainframe computers are all linked together to allow users to access tremendous sources of information. Personal computers can be connected to data files and other equipment stored remotely, somewhere in a company's building, and information is accessed with the touch of your finger right from your own computer terminal. Another fun new thing that you can do with your computer, thanks to new advances in the field of information technology, is to bypass your phone to make long distance calls around the world, thanks to brand new state-of-the-art software. So many new things are on the horizon in terms of what information technology brings to your everyday life.

FIELDS WITHIN THE FIELD

At this point, you are probably curious to know more about the specialized fields within the field of information technology. So let's go!

Communications

When you hear the word "communications," what does it make you think of? Do you think of people talking to one another? How? On the phone? Perhaps you think of people writing letters or sending e-mails back and forth. Communications is a vast field that involves anything in which two or more people correspond and share information. For the purpose of this book on information technology, the field of communications that deals with data, computer software, and hardware is most important. Communications using computers rely on software and hardware to link computers together. Often the computers are very far apart and the information being communicated must travel vast distances to get to where it needs to go. Someone has to design the networks for the information to travel across. These people are communications specialists: the communications manager and the analysts that work for the communications manager. If you are a communications specialist, you will need to be proficient in computer languages, software applications, and the many different devices actually used for communication. Not only do these people design the data networks, but they also install and operate these links so that the information can actually travel along the network to get to where it has to go. In other words, they are responsible for all aspects of making sure the data network is put together and running properly. Not only do they design and code the programs, but they are responsible for testing them to make sure that the programs work efficiently. They are then responsible for debugging the programs, documenting the work they have done, and getting the software program up and running. Once the program is in use and functioning properly, the communications specialist is in charge of keeping an eye on it and making sure that it continues to do what it is supposed to. They may have to tweak the system, or modify it as needs change. In recent years, the area of communications has grown, creating more jobs in information technology.

Local area networks (LANs) and wide area networks (WANs) are two of the relatively new advances in network technology. A LAN can be as simple as two computers connected together. Most companies rely on LANs. LANs provide employees of a company with the tools they need to increase work productivity and efficiency, while also providing ways for the employees to better perform their jobs, share information throughout the office, and communicate within the organization without ever having to leave their desks. A WAN, by contrast, can span the globe. Some people consider the Internet to be the largest WAN of all. (LANs and WANs will be discussed in greater detail later on.)

The people who work on these networks are the network engineer, who actually designs the networks and does studies and tests to see if the networks are working the way they need to be; the network manager, whose job it is to coordinate how the networks are used; the network analyst, who analyzes the network system to see how well it is working; and the network administrator, who sees to the day-to-day needs of the network and helps the users (people who use the computers on the network) when they have problems.

Computer Programmer

The computer programmer's job is crucial. He or she is responsible for writing detailed sets of instructions that follow the specific needs prescribed by the systems analyst. This particular kind of writing is called coding. The programs written by the computer programmer are made up of a series of logical steps for the computer to follow in order to properly process the data into information that can be used in whatever way it needs to be. There are more than one thousand computer programming languages. You will not have to know all of them, of course. But perhaps you recognize the names of some of the most widely used programming languages. FORTRAN, BASIC, COBOL, and Pascal are some of the most common and also among the oldest of the programming languages. If you are already familiar with COBOL, you are ahead of the game because 65 percent of all corporate systems still run on COBOL. Today C and C++ are two of the most commonly used languages for the newer computer programs. In fact, they are not only widely used for business applications, they are also used for computer games as well. Recently, computer programmers have been using languages like Visual Basic and Visual C++, which are designed to help the programmer code faster and easier. Computer programmers should be familiar with the most common programming languages, including DB2 and other database software.

If you are leaning toward a career as a computer programmer, you ought to have a strong knack for detail. The smallest details in this area can mean the difference between something that works and something that does not function. One single misplaced period or comma could cause an entire program to fail. A system malfunction could cause a great inconvenience or even a tragic, life-threatening disaster such as a plane crash. So the computer programmer must be able to track even the smallest of details when he or she is checking a program for errors. This is called debugging, and it usually involves testing the system using sample data to see if it works properly.

Another responsibility of the computer programmer is writing specific instructions to explain to someone else how to use the software that he or she has just written. However, sometimes a technical writer gets to do this job. One way or another, the computer programmer has a great deal of responsibility. He or she may work alone or on a team. Writing a program may take a short period of time, like a few hours or days, or it may take a great deal of time, like a year or more, depending on what is needed. If you decide that you would like to become a computer programmer, you also get to decide what kind of programmer you want to be. You can choose from a list of subspecialties that includes maintenance programmers, scientific applications programmers, business applications programmers, and operating systems programmers.

Maintenance programmers are responsible for the upkeep of the system. They will constantly work to make a system better and more efficient. Debugging is a regular function of this position as well. It may sound like a simple job, but it is not. It is pretty complex and takes a wealth of knowledge and skills. You will need to be proficient in your debugging skills as well as your programming skills. Although much of this skill and technique comes with experience, recent graduates are often hired into this area so that they can be taught on the job by veterans of the field.

Scientific applications programmers must have great math skills. Their work is very mathematical, as they are responsible for the development of the programs that solve scientific or engineering problems. For this job you will need to have at least a bachelor's degree in math, engineering, or science, but a master's degree is preferred. You should also have a strong background in programming languages such as FORTRAN, Assembler, Pascal, and C, experience with programming for operating systems, and exposure to personal computer hardware as well as large-scale computer hardware.

Business applications programmers do many different things. They may be responsible for routine events such as customer billing. They may develop programs for users, or they may develop programs for complex systems within a company. Although a recent trend in the development of better business software packages has lessened the demand for programmers in this area to a certain extent, there are still plenty of employment opportunities in the area of personal computers and computers in smaller commercial systems. You may also be responsible for the support of other functions, such as communications, databases, graphics, and operating systems.

Operating systems programmers do highly technical work. They are responsible for writing sets of instructions that make computer programming easier. The sets of instructions are called the operating systems. They control how the entire computer system works and usually become part of the computer's permanent memory system so that everything continues to work together smoothly. It is therefore important for the operating systems programmer to understand all of the inner workings of the computer. An exciting part of this job is the opportunity to adapt existing programming languages to fit the needs of something new, or even coming up with and writing new programming languages. For this job you will need a degree in computer science. You will also need to know how computer circuits are structured, which is called computer architecture.

CASE Tools

CASE stand for Computer-Aided Software Engineering. These tools are actually software packages that are used to generate specific computer coding according to the specifications of a particular company, as prescribed by a computer programmer. CASE tools have done a lot to reduce the amount of time that is needed by computer programmers to create new programs when companies need them or to revise existing programs to keep them updated so that they continue to meet a company's needs. One of the biggest expenses in the field of information technology is in programming. One of the reasons for this expense is that it takes quite a bit of time to write most computer programs and then additional time is required to debug the programs and get them ready to be used. Another problem is that often more than one company needs a program with similar but not exactly the same specifications, and so even more time is spent adapting the programs to meet each individual company's requirements. CASE tools change all of that. Many companies now use CASE tools to develop their own software without incurring the great cost and time of utilizing the services of computer programmers.

Computer Sales and Service Representative

Someone has to sell all the computers and the software and hardware for them. This person provides the essential link between the people who create computers and the people who utilize the services provided by computers. Once the computer programmers and other experts have produced the computer software and hardware systems, these things have to be marketed to the companies or individuals for which they were created. The computer sales representative is the person responsible for going out and marketing the computer products and getting them sold to the people who need them. Certainly for this job some direct knowledge of computers and the systems you are selling is necessary. It is equally important to have a lot of self-confidence and a good sense of how to talk to people to help them understand what you are selling and how it can be of benefit to them to purchase it.

Often the computer sales representative has several other responsibilities. For example, after the product is sold to a company, the computer sales representative may wear the hat of field engineer and become responsible for installing the software and the hardware and providing the periodic maintenance necessary for everything to continue to run smoothly.

The computer service representative's job is to help the company solve its day-to-day troubles as they occur within the system. Sometimes the computer sales representative takes on this responsibility as well. Another task that the computer sales representative may encounter is training. He or she may be the person who not only installs the new system for the company but also trains the employees at the company in how to use the system. This part of the job may entail varying degrees of travel, depending on the company you work for. The annual salary at this point becomes quite competitive to compensate for the great deal of knowledge and expertise you must have both in terms of marketing the products and then training people to use them. Management positions are not far off as a computer sales representative or a computer service representative climbs the corporate ladder. To read about a real-life computer software and training professional, skip ahead to chapter 11 and read about Jay Leib, a director of software sales and training, but be sure to come back when you are finished.

Data Service Organizations

Systems analysts, data entry operators, computer programmers, and service and sales representatives often find employment in the area of data service organizations. Data service organizations are companies that do one of two things: They either add additional computer capacity to companies that do not have enough on their own systems, or they provide all of the computer data processing for small companies that have not grown large enough to have computer systems of their own yet. Many companies, especially the smaller ones, worry that some of the computer equipment currently available will become outdated or even obsolete in just a short period of time. They are concerned that they will be wasting valuable company dollars if they invest in such equipment. So instead, the companies employ data service organizations to keep their records and maintain their information for them. Many data service organizations also employ specialists who do systems analysis, documentation, systems design, and provide employee training as well.

Database Management

Database managers arrange databases so that they work efficiently. There are many ways to arrange a database, just as there are many ways to arrange a closet, but some ways make it much easier for people to find what they are looking for. A database, as you most likely know already, is a set of related data that is used by programmers and systems analysts to produce information that a particular company needs. A database administrator is responsible for analyzing exactly what it is that the company needs in terms of information. Then he or she coordinates the way the data is collected, organizes that data into user friendly databases, and stores the information so that the other programmers and analysts can easily get to it. The database administrator is also responsible for maintaining the database system and keeping it up-to-date. It is also necessary for the database administrator to provide security measures and guidelines. If there is too much work for the database administrator to do alone, he or she may employ a database analyst and librarian.

Expert Systems

All of the areas of information technology employ their own experts or specialists. But in this particular area, the computers themselves are the experts. You have probably heard the term "artificial intelligence." This refers to computers "knowing" how to do things and being able to figure things out that have previously been done only by human beings. Expert systems are designed to simulate creative human thinking as if the computers are experts in a particular field. Then they provide information and assist with decision making. Of course, an expert system is just that, a system. In no way does it actually replace a human expert. It merely helps the human expert to be as efficient as possible when it comes to decision making and problem solving.

For example, a doctor might input a set of symptoms and the computer in turn helps the doctor figure out possible diagnoses, suggests potential treatments, and provides further information on available drug therapies. Of course, a doctor could go to books and periodicals to research the same information, or he or she could talk with other doctors and solicit advice and suggestions. Doctors still do work this way, of course, but if a doctor does not have any other doctors available to confer with, or simply lacks the time to do the exhaustive research necessary to quickly and adequately treat a sick patient, expert systems will help the doctor get the necessary information in the shortest time possible. Expert systems are used in many other industries as well, providing information from data analysis to accident analysis, to the projected need for supplies and when to purchase them. At this time, there are not many human experts in the area of expert systems so there are many jobs available in this up-and-coming field. In fact, computer professionals who possess these expert systems programming skills are among corporations' most-wanted today.

Information Technology Management

Wherever you work, someone has to run the information technology department. Are you cut out to be the manager? Managers work in various areas and at different levels within an office. The manager of the information technology department is the person who assigns the right computer person to the right task. Managers often arrange for user training and coordinate the distribution of new technologies throughout the company. The managers are also responsible for tasks such as hiring personnel, budgeting projects, planning, supervising workers and projects, and evaluating the work of other employees. Managers are given the authority to oversee these areas.

In order to move up the ladder into a management position you will need to be in command of certain skills. Among the most important skills are communication skills and decision-making skills. You will also need to understand all aspects of the business in which you are employed. You will need to be comfortable with the management style of the office, and you will have to have a good working relationship with the other employees of the company. Working well with people and having respect for those you work with, not to mention having their respect, are all very important characteristics for a manager to possess. Information managers often require the help of assistants to keep them updated on the latest technology and how to use the technology in their office. These assistants are called consultants. Some consultants work in the same company, and others are hired to come in from the outside.

With the right skills, it is possible to move up into a pretty high position in a company. At the very top is the chief information officer (CIO). This is a high-level and very important executive position within a company. The CIO is in charge of all information functions within the company, and he or she plays an extremely important role in corporate strategic planning. Beneath the CIO is the director of information. Beneath the director is a lateral list of management positions: communications manager (who works above the network manager), database manager, director of systems development (who coordinates the manager of systems analysis, the manager of applications programming, and the manager of operating systems programming), the manager of operations, the manager of word processing (who manages the word processing supervisor), and the director of security. These are the key information science management positions within a given company.

Not all companies will necessarily have all of these positions. Most of the management positions today are high level. This is because the middle management positions become more and more obsolete as the computers themselves become more efficient and the upper-level managers become more and more able to access information for themselves via the computer. Managers must possess competent managerial skills in addition to what they must know about the technical aspects of what their company does. Obviously the higher level managers must have a great deal of managerial skills, whereas the lower-level manager really needs a good set of technical skills. They are the ones who are working right in the heart of it all and dealing with the new technologies. If the technology is what interests you the most, a managerial position would probably hold very little interest for you.

Internet and Intranet

You have certainly heard of—and probably used—the Internet. It is the international electronic network that allows people around the world to communicate with one another, as well as access information through a system of Web sites about almost anything you can think of. But do you wonder what an Intranet is? An Intranet is like the Internet, with a difference. Where the Internet can be accessed by anyone who has a computer and a dial-up connection, the Intranet can be accessed only by people who are directly linked to that particular Intranet system. It is like having an Internet just for a single company or institution. For example, a company may have set up their own Intranet for the benefit of their employees. Their Intranet might give out company information such as the comings and going of employees, or perhaps information needed by employees to do their jobs better. In other words, the Intranet is a source of computer-based information for people within a particular system. The Internet and the World Wide Web, as well as the Intranet system, are all relatively new aspects of information technology. As you can imagine, their debut on the scene has opened up a whole new realm of computer and information technology jobs.

The people who work on the Internet, the Intranet, and Web sites have some fun job titles, the best of which is Webmaster. Other job titles include Web developer, Web programmer, Intranet network administrator, and Web user support consultant. Because many companies are now using the Internet to market their products, these companies must employ experts and specialists to put together their Web sites for them. If this end of information technology interests you, you may find yourself doing any number of different tasks. You will set up the Web site, and provide links to other areas within the site or to other Internet sites using Java, HTML, and Web browsers. You may be responsible for setting up the security necessary to keep computer criminals from entering and destroying your Web site. You may do these tasks within the company as a full-time employee working only on the company's site, or you may work for a company that specializes in setting up Web sites for other companies.

This is a growing field. Almost every company out there has or will soon have their own Web site, and many jobs are available. Companies look to hire managers, analysts, designers, content providers, and researchers to make their Web sites interesting to look at and easy to use, and then to get the Web sites up and running. Another interesting job that uses the Internet is that of Internet researcher. Just about anything a person could possibly want to look up or research can potentially be found on the Internet. Weather, maps and directions, airfares, travel destinations, sports events, entertainment schedules and tickets, historical and political information, medical and scientific updates, recipes, advice columns, job openings, new and used cars, home shopping—they are all available on the Internet. If you are the kind of person who loves to "surf the net" and gather information, and if the whole Internet experience fascinates you, then perhaps this is the road you should take to set your career on track. If you have a knack for doing research and are good at looking things up and figuring out the best way to find something in particular, you may want to establish yourself as an Internet researcher. To read about a real-life Internet specialist, see chapter 5 about Wade Brown.

Networks

The people who work with networks are in the same field as the people who work in communications. Almost every company out there uses a network of one sort or another to maintain its day-to-day operations. Think about all of the computers out there. Stores, banks, airlines, and just about every other large industry uses computer terminals to accomplish what is referred to as on-line transaction processing (OLTP). Networks, as you probably already know, are the electronic pathways that connect the company's computer terminals to a larger main computer and to each other.

There are two basic types of networks, depending on their size and how much distance they cover. A small network, one that is based within a company or an office building, is called a local area network (LAN). The larger network, which reaches a large geographical area, is referred to as a wide area network (WAN). The reason these networks are in such widespread use today is that when computers are linked to each other to share information, workers increase their individual productivity, that is, do their jobs better and more efficiently. E-mail was created to enhance this information sharing, as it is certainly easier and faster to send an e-mail than an office memo. Employees can use their LAN system to communicate not only with each another, but also with other machines in the office, such as the printer, copy machines, and data storage devices. All of the company's information can be stored in the main or central computer and employees can access information as they need it, without ever getting up from their desks. You have undoubtedly already used an e-mail system at some point. But have you used any of the more advanced modes of communication? For example, instant messages are faster than e-mails. They allow two or more people to type in messages and deliver them instantly. It is almost like having a telephone conversation, but the parties are typing instead of talking. But if talking suits you better, you may be interested in working to help create the LAN systems that allow transmission of voice, videos, print, graphics, and even three-dimensional animated digital graphics. Communication possibilities using LANs and WANs are absolutely endless.

Operations

Operations is an area that involves several levels of employees. Data entry operators are the people responsible for accurately entering the data into the system. This job generally entails sitting at a computer and typing in the information. There are also the people who work as computer operators, and they are responsible for setting up the computer and all of the equipment needed to maintain the system. You may be in charge of things like mounting and removing tapes, printer forms, and disks, monitoring existing jobs in progress, or troubleshooting problems that may come up. The production control operators make sure that the work goes where it is supposed to go after it is complete. The manager of operations is responsible for overseeing the computer operators. For a career in operations, you will be able to get most of the training you need while you are in high school. You may also train at a vocational school or at a community college. Much of your experience will be gained while you are on the job, however. As you gain more knowledge and experience, you will likely advance to higher levels within the area of operations. If, however, you aspire to advance up to the position of manager of operations, you ought to stay in school and earn your bachelor's degree before joining the workforce.

Personal Computer User Services

Many people in many different fields are now using computers to do their work. From word processing to information retrieval, people in large companies as well as people who work from personal computers in their own homes rely on computers to get their work done. A personal computer user services specialist is needed to maintain these computers so that the users do not miss even a day of work because of computer problems. A day of missed work can mean a missed deadline. So the personal computer user services specialist works with both the systems development professionals and the management information technology professionals and other users within the company to keep things running smoothly. Making sure that the computers are capable of performing necessary tasks and coordinating the computer uses within the office are essential activities. It is also usually the personal computer user services specialists who teach the company's employees how to use their computers and the systems available on them.

Personal Computers

If you have your own computer, you have a personal computer. Your personal computer, or PC, probably came with a lot of software already installed on it. Perhaps there was a personal banking program, a word processing program, a system to help you connect to the Internet, a connector to your printer, and possibly some other systems. Perhaps you also purchased software to plan trips, play games, or any number of other things that you want your computer to do. Someone had to create all of these programs and then install them before you got your computer, or put them on CDs so that you could buy them and install them yourself. This is the area called software development.

Then there are the people who maintain your computer after you buy it. They offer technical support over the phone or via the Internet when you have questions about what you are doing or how to do it, or when you are having a problem setting something up or trying to troubleshoot an application that won't work. On the other end of your phone you will find a computer expert who is able to diagnose and troubleshoot without even seeing your computer. Other experts in this area of computers and information technology may find employment within a company and do all of the maintenance and troubleshooting for the computers used by the employees of that company. For any company that uses a large number of computers, it is a wise move to employ a specialist or a team of specialists to maintain the company's network. After all, if even one computer goes down, that could mean that one person cannot get any work done all day, which could in turn affect other employees working on the same project. Suddenly a whole day is wasted. So having full-time computer specialists, analysts, and programmers working in-house is a great advantage for any company that relies on computers to get its work done.

Security

Security is a very important aspect of information technology and computers. For without security not only could everything stored on computers be accessed by anyone, but anyone who is vindictive enough can come in and wipe out everything on any given system. Such a disaster could mean the ruin of a business. In order to keep the vast amounts of available information on the network safe from people who wish to inflict harm, security personnel are employed to set up systems for protecting the networks and databases. The security specialist sets up protection against such invasions as computer viruses, credit card number theft, personal information invasions, as well as natural disasters like fire or flood damage. The director of security is charged with overseeing the security specialists as they work on protecting the data and the computer's resources. To do this job, you will need a strong background in both systems analysis and computer programming, as well as some experience with information systems auditing. If disaster recovery sounds exciting to you, you will want to work on your operations skills as well as your communications skills. You may move into the director position eventually and so you may find it helpful to be well versed in both areas.

The security personnel for a company may work within the company or they may be employed by an outside company to come in and do security maintenance. Often the security checks they do are not scheduled. Of course, company management is always aware that these checks will occur. Another security check that may be run within a company's computer system is a virus scan. Many virus scans are activated by the personal computer's user at his or her convenience. Others are set up by security personnel and are randomly activated. Either way, it is important to have the security system well in place to protect the work of the company's employees as well as any "company secrets," things the company may deem confidential and not for public viewing, such as employee records or sales figures.

Systems Analyst

If you become a systems analyst, your job will be to design new computer systems or improve the systems that already exist. But what exactly do we mean when we refer to a system? Well, a system is a group of things, namely people and machines, plus programs and procedures (specific ways of doing things) that are set up to get certain things done in the most effective way. Systems analyst is really a fancy term for problem solver. If you are good at taking things apart and figuring out what is going wrong, this may be the area for you. As a systems analyst, you would be responsible for analyzing the problems or analyzing what information people in the company need. Once you have this information in hand, you will design the necessary programs. These programs will create special patterns for the information to move from a source of data to the computer where the information is needed.

Another responsibility of the systems analyst is to plan how the information gets distributed. He or she makes this plan based on how the information is going to be used within the company or the organization. To design and maintain a really good system of information flow, the systems analyst has to work very closely with managers, accountants, and other groups of people who use the system. Sometimes these people are coordinated into a team to get these types of jobs done. The systems analyst may work within this team to help figure out what the company's needs are in terms of information and also figure out what kinds of problems might come up. This is why it is important for the systems analyst to have some understanding about what the company does and how it works. An understanding of various departments, such as marketing and accounting, is of great help to the systems analyst.

It is also necessary to have good skills in the area of communications. It is important to be able to communicate effectively with your coworkers in order to keep information flowing smoothly. After a while on the job, a systems analyst will probably move up the ladder, and his or her job will involve work in the areas of management or supervisory duties. Responsibilities may include such things as scheduling, estimating, controlling time, and accepting responsibility for projects. The systems analyst is also responsible for educating the programmers about the computer hardware. It will be your job to explain the requirements of the system, as well as what the computer hardware is capable of doing for the programmers. The programmers need to know what plan to follow when they are writing the software for the computer systems. In some cases, depending on the company you are working for, the programmer may also be you. Your job title would be systems analyst/programmer. Whether or not you work for a company in which you have this dual job title or you are only a systems analyst working with the programmers, you will have to have a good understanding of the responsibilities of the programmer. Most systems analysts start out as programmers.

Systems Development and Programming

Many jobs fall under this heading. The two most notable jobs are systems analyst and computer programmer, both of which you have already read about. Both jobs have to do with developing the systems that create instructions for different things that computers do. You may have heard the word "software" before, too. Software is the technical word for computer instructions. The people who write the information contained within the software are professional experts in the areas of systems development and programming.

Word Processing

If you are a good typist but lack formal education, word processing might be the field for you. Word processors type text into computers using word processing programs to produce documents. Word processing programs allow you to do things such as delete information, insert new information, rearrange paragraphs or sentences, highlight, underline, or italicize. When a word processor is done with his or her work, that work can be stored for retrieval at a later time. When you start out as a word processor, you will work at an entry level, learning the job and becoming proficient at what you do. You may eventually advance on up to a supervisor or word processing manager position. If you have a lot of patience and a tolerance for doing the same kind of routine work over a long period of time, data entry and word processing may be the direction for you to take.

2

What to Study in School

For any career, it is good to have what is referred to as a well-rounded background. All this means is that you have exposed yourself to different subjects and have some knowledge and interest in different things. Of course, your specialty will be in an area of information technology, but it always helps to be familiar with other areas. For example, having some experience dealing with other people will be helpful if your company sends you out to work with clients. Your interpersonal skills will be very valuable. A panel of experts who currently work in the field of information technology were asked what focus high school students should take, and this is what they recommend.

Pay attention in all of your classes, even in the ones that you do not like very much. One of the most important and valuable skills in information science is the ability to learn new things quickly, and then to be able to use what you learn. I also recommend that anyone interested in pursuing information science get a part-time job tutoring other students at your school. Tutoring other people is a very good experience. Having the skills to tutor will help you out since being able to communicate ideas in a clear way to someone who does not understand is something that you will have to do a lot of as someone working in information science.

—Wade Brown, Internet specialist

Students wishing to pursue information science as a career ought to be taking a lot of math classes and then subjects involving logic and analytical skills.

—Nagesh Reddy, senior consultant

High school students who plan to pursue information science as a career should take a heavy curriculum of math and sciences. I cannot stress that enough. In fact, I would suggest more math classes than science classes. The field of computers is surprisingly heavy in math. Students must not ignore the sciences, though. Furthermore, I recommend you take electronics courses. The more you know about the electronics aspect of computers and information science—how things actually work—the more marketable you will be when you are looking for a job. There is one other class that I cannot emphasize enough—TYPING! Typing was the most useful class I ever took. I believe typing ought to be required of every student when they first enter high school. In a field where your hands are constantly at the keyboard, basic typing skills are an absolute must.

—Ed Kuehl, information technology manager

I would recommend studying the newer technologies, such as HTML, JavaScript, Java, IIS, VB, and Domino. The information technology industry is moving toward the Internet and Web applications, so if you understand these technologies you will always be in demand! Of course, to begin with an understanding of computer basics is very important as well!

—John Hutton, senior consultant

I am not certain that a specific subject is as important as taking time to learn about locating information, reviewing it, organizing it, and presenting it in a logical and orderly fashion. I think that as a student, you can choose to learn this process in whichever classroom subject you enjoy the most, whether it is history, English, science, mathematics, or anything else you have a great deal of interest in. Become comfortable with the Internet's search capabilities. Listen to the news and read about the new trends that are occurring in the computer industry. Get comfortable with computers and learn the applications that have become standard. Explore the applications that interest you, such as JavaScript or graphics.

—Denise Pagel, Web administrator

The most important class to take in high school is computer programming, especially the language called C. Another very important subject is math. Students should take math courses at least up through calculus. There is quite a deal of math in this field, believe it or not. In college, the best degrees for this field are in engineering.

—Adam Frederickson, video game designer
and small business owner

High school was not exactly my favorite four years, but I am very glad that I had the opportunity to take a few computer courses while I was there. I also think that all the classes I took in one way or another helped me to become the well-rounded person I am now.

—Samantha Hoffman, transfer coordinator
and data mapper

35

Obviously, someone thinking about pursuing information science should look into taking any and all computer classes that are being offered. I feel there are actually two sides to information science: the support side and the technical side. The people who work on the support side are the ones who deal with people using the computer systems. The technical people are sometimes called "feed 'em under the door techs" (that is, they have very poor people skills and would rather work on technology alone). Students who are interested in working on the support side of the field should consider taking a public speaking class or an acting class because you have to be good at working in front of people and these kinds of classes will give you that advantage. If you are more interested in the technical side of the field, take a shop class or an art class. These classes will help you because a tech needs to be good with his or her hands.

—Matt Helms, desktop support supervisor

Take anything to do with computers, but especially programming. Math and typing will help a great deal.

—Michael Radomsky, executive vice president

I would recommend that students take any type of computer science classes their high school offers. Internet technology and classes like that, which deal with the latest technology, would be especially helpful. You have to gain some business sense as well. I recommend this because, although you may be thinking that you just want to enter a technical field, you will still find yourself needing to know how to handle yourself from a business standpoint. It does not hurt to increase your social skills along with your presentation skills so that you are effective in communicating your true knowledge. If you cannot communicate effectively, no one will really get a good understanding of what you know and are trying to teach.

—Michael Jaltuch, information science specialist

I would tell students to be well rounded. Study a lot of things. But get as much hands-on computer experience as possible.

—Jay Leib, director of software sales and training

If your school offers it, I recommend that you take computer science courses as well as math and accounting classes. Research has also shown that people who do well in the languages also succeed in information science, so I would suggest that you get your feet wet in French or Spanish or whatever foreign language your high school offers.

—Barbara Radomsky, manager and small business owner

Obviously, you will want to take as many computer and information science classes as your high school offers and you can comfortably fit into your schedule. However, do not be so eager to fill up on computer classes that you neglect all other classes. Math and science are very important for certain areas of information science. Language arts and English skills will help you communicate both in writing and verbally. These are important classes, too, as you will want to learn to communicate in a manner that highlights your skills, talents, and abilities. After all, what good will it do you if you have all the computer skills in the world, but you lack the ability to put together a proper sentence in which you can explain what you know? Good grammar and spelling are always important skills to have, especially when you are putting together your initial cover letter and résumé to find your job. Public speaking and drama classes will help you to overcome any inhibitions you may have about speaking in front of a group. In other words, your computer classes are important, but so are all of your other classes. Remember that you want to be well rounded. It will make you more interesting, for sure!

3

Do I Have What It Takes?

The following is a help wanted ad from the information technology section of a large Chicago newspaper. Does the job described here appeal to you? Do you have the skills necessary to fit into this company's work environment?

We are looking for an energetic individual with excellent interpersonal skills to support our sales staff. Functions include Internet sourcing, résumé review, phone screening, in-person interviewing, and ultimately matching technical candidates to client needs. The successful candidate will be degreed or have past exposure to technical recruiting environments. Must thrive in a fast-paced environment and have the ability to multitask without losing primary focus. We offer a cohesive and supportive working environment, and the opportunity to work in one of the hottest industries in the country. Potential candidates should have a thorough understanding of the Internet and Internet search engines. Skills using general office PC software a must. You should be very familiar with e-mail, IE4, Netscape, Word, Excel, and so forth. In addition, any hardware, networking, telemarketing, or human resources background is a plus.

Information technology managers are looking to hire people who possess a certain base of skills, experience, and knowledge. Do you have experience already? In what area? The most in-demand experience areas are network technologies, database, telecommunications, client-server systems, expert systems, multimedia systems, and OOPS and CASE applications.

You may find your information technology job from a help wanted advertisement in the classified section of your local newspaper. You may hear about a job opening from a friend or relative who already works in the field. While you are still in school, you may be recruited by a company who has seen your work, or your career counselor may help you find your job. Sometimes finding a great job is just a matter of good luck, that is, happening to be in the right place at the right time. People land jobs in all different ways.

I was offered my current job because I did some freelance business with the guy who eventually hired me. Honestly, I get a job offer every couple of months from somebody. In my region I am fairly well known for being pretty good at what I do.

—Wade Brown, Internet specialist

I learned about my job from my father. He has been working in the industry of information science for almost forty years. I have always loved computers and I was always amazed at what they can do. In learning that from my father, I also managed to educate myself in school.

—Michael Jaltuch, information science specialist

I was not really looking to change jobs when this new job was presented to me. A guy I had worked with for about four years at my former job left his position about three years ago. Shortly after he left he started calling me. We had at one point worked on a team together, before I was a team manager. He knew what kind of work I did and he was eager to have me join him at the new company. He knew I had completed my master's degree and he also knew that the company I was working for was pretty far from my home. He persisted and finally persuaded me to come look at the company he was working for. I liked what I saw, but at first I really had no interest in changing jobs. By the time I thought about moving to a job closer to home, this guy was already working on getting me to move over to his company. So in fact I never even had to send out my résumés to any businesses in an attempt to find work closer to home. The job really came to me.

—Ed Kuehl, information technology master

I heard about my current job from a friend of mine who already worked for the company. She recommended me to the human resources director when she heard that the position was available. She suggested that I apply because she thought the job description sounded like a position I would be good at and I would enjoy. She was right!

—Julia James, Web coordinator

If you are having a difficult time finding work, you may want to consider hooking up with a temporary

41

employment service. Temp services, as they are called, will place you in temporary positions with companies that are looking to fill a temporary need. Some temp jobs last only one day, while others last for quite some time and eventually turn into full-time positions.

My original information science job was working at a bank. I got the job through a temp agency that I had been doing work for when I moved to the city. The temp job eventually turned into a full-time job, which I stayed with for a couple of years until basically I outgrew it in terms of my skills and what they were willing to pay me. Once I outgrew the position at the bank, I moved to the mortgage company where I still work now. I actually heard about this job from a colleague of mine who had also worked at the bank and then moved to the mortgage company. She called me and told me that there was a position opening up that I might qualify for. Sure enough, my skills and experience did fill their requirements and I was hired. I have been here ever since.

—Samantha Hoffman, transfer
coordinator and data mapper

This help wanted ad appeared in the *Chicago Tribune*. We have changed the name of the company.

ABC Interactive is seeking an Internet Producer to build and maintain their Web site. This position will be located directly at the television station in Chicago. In this role, you will be responsible for creating on-line content, including posting news stories and headlines,

*updating sports and weather, and creating program-
ming information updates. Additionally, you will coordinate the creation of on-line content with our company. Candidates should possess a college degree with
emphasis on journalism, communications, or media, or
equivalent work experience. This position requires
knowledge of HTML and related Internet languages
(JavaScript, Java, CGI, Perl); graphics and multimedia (Photoshop, Illustrator); strong editing skills;
and solid communication skills.*

Here's another ad for a network technology analyst.

*XYZ Information Systems has an exciting
career opportunity for an experienced information
networks professional as a network technology analyst. Qualified candidates should possess knowledge
of secure Internet protocols and firewalls; ability to
develop and implement security policies and solutions; experience with Internet services and emerging technologies; understanding of multiprotocol
and multi-OS environments; Unix system adminis-
tration experience; excellent project management
skills; two to five years professional experience in
network analysis, design, and support; and a degree
in computer science or experience in a related technical discipline.*

*In return, we offer a competitive annual salary and
benefits package. Interested professionals should submit
a résumé and annual salary requirement to our
résumé-processing center.*

*I had been working part-time at a nonprofit com-
munity center near my home while my children were*

young. The wife of the chairman of the board at my current place of employment happened to do volunteer work at the community center where I was working. She knew the quality of work I could do and that my kids were old enough for me to return to a nine to five job, so she recommended me to her husband. I think I was the right person, in the right place, with the right skills, at the right time.

—Denise Pagel, Web administrator

This advertisement seeking a WAN/LAN analyst appeared in the *Chicago Tribune*'s on-line help wanted section. The name of the company has been changed.

Triple A Information Systems supports the Daily Newspaper *and other company-related business units from the historic* Daily Newspaper *building downtown. The networking team has an exciting career opportunity that would include wide area and local area network design/operations, policies and solutions for routing, switching and other infrastructure development. Experience with protocols (IP, IPX, Apple Talk), network monitoring tools (Network Associates-Sniffer technology, HP-OV), and CISCO routing and switching is needed for this tremendous opportunity. Additionally, the ideal candidate should have a college degree or equivalent education. Formal CISCO training or certification is a plus. The career path and opportunity to learn emerging technologies is endless. Triple A Information Systems offers not only a highly competitive annual salary but also an exceptional benefits package that includes 401K, employee stock ownership plan and purchase plan, tuition reimbursement, and flexible benefits package.*

I found my current job while I was browsing the Internet one day. I was not even looking for a job really, rather I was just looking to see what was out there. But the information was there, so I jumped on it. I was even able to apply for the job via the Internet. Another fine example of information science at work!

—Nagesh Reddy, senior consultant

I was recruited by posting my résumé on a Web site.

—Jay Leib, director of software sales and training

This Internet software developer position also comes from on-line sources. Again, the company name has been changed.

The applicant will be responsible for designing, implementing, deploying, and maintaining our major Web site and other multimedia/Internet products. Requires two to three years programming experience and hands-on SQL and familiarity with relational database concepts. Should have an undergraduate degree in computer science, MIS, or related field or equivalent related experience. Must have experience in the design, implementation, deployment, and maintenance of multimedia/Internet products; TCL, SQL, and Perl programming using high-end database publishing tolls writing scripts. Must have strong understanding and experience with the UNIX environment and familiarity with software design and development methodologies and practices. Must have knowledge of the Web and awareness of the Internet industry and associated technology; skills to evaluate, test, and recommend new emerging Internet technologies; ability to be available twenty-four-seven on an emergency basis.

Reading these actual help wanted ads should give you some perspective about exactly what companies look for when they are hiring new employees.

I learned about my current job from the Chicago Tribune*'s on-line ad service. However, I had also looked for jobs on www.monster.com, but I found that the* Chicago Tribune *had better regional coverage.*

—Matt Helms, desktop support supervisor

As you continue your research into the field of information technology and determine whether or not this is the right field for you, you may want to start by asking yourself some questions.

- Do I like to work with computers?
- Am I good at working with computers?
- Do I have the skills I need to work in the field of information technology?
- Is there a certain aspect or area of information technology that particularly appeals to me?
- How much more education will I need to get the job I want?
- Am I willing to further my education in order to qualify for the job I want?
- Will I be able to make enough money in the field?

- Do I work well with other people?
- Am I cut out for a management position?
- Am I a leader or a follower?
- Do I have good communication skills?
- Do I learn things quickly?
- Can I adapt quickly and easily to changes in the industry?

These are just some of the questions to ask yourself. There are no set answers for these questions. Rather, you can use your individual answers to help you determine whether or not you personally feel that a career in information technology would be a good career move for you.

I would like to offer a piece of advice to students who are considering pursuing a career in information science: Possessing both a willingness and the ability to learn is just as important, if not more important, than technical experience and knowledge. Since information science is such a rapidly evolving field, flexibility and adaptability are extremely attractive qualities to possess.

—Matt Helms, desktop support supervisor

Finding a job may be the easiest thing you have ever done, or it may present some challenges. Here are some things to remember when you are looking for a job.

- Present yourself in a professional manner when you are interviewing.
- Have confidence in your skills and knowledge.
- Do not lie or exaggerate the extent of your skills and knowledge to make yourself look more qualified than you really are.

- Show up on time for your interview.
- Bring an extra copy of your résumé to every interview.

This is a job description posted on the Internet by a company looking to hire an information technologist project manager.

The Information Technologist Project Manager hired by this company will be responsible for managing and coordinating enhancements to an existing installation and the project functions related to a new software implementation as well. The ideal candidate for the job will meet the following requirements:

- *Must have experience in large ERP system implementations*

- *Must have experience in structured project methodologies*

- *Must possess technical skills and aptitude for this type of work*

- *Must have fluent understanding of business processes*

- *Must have three years of project management experience*

- *Good verbal and communication skills*

- *Previous ERP systems experience*

- *Information technology knowledge, databases, operating systems, networks, and hardware*

• Must be able to work in a team environment

• Must be able to work independently, if required

Look at this list of job titles taken from the *Chicago Tribune*'s Sunday job section under the heading Computer/Information Technology. If you were to visit the Web site you would be able to click on any one of the entries on the list and read about the currently available jobs under that heading. It is truly amazing to note just how many different jobs fall under the heading of information technology. It is also a comfort for anyone considering entering the field to see the great number of available job opportunities.

- Analyst
- Analyst/Customer Resources
- Application Development Manager
- Applications Specialist
- Associate Analyst
- Associate Producer
- Circulation Systems Analyst
- CISCO WAN/LAN Analyst
- Computer Operator
- Database Analyst
- Director of Advanced Broadcast Technology
- Director of Computing Technologies
- Director of Core Technology
- Director of Quality
- Director of Technology/Electronic Program Guides
- Executive Producer
- Executive Producer/Electronic Program Guides
- Interactive Producer
- Internet Applications Developer

- Internet Producer
- Internet Producer/Affiliate Sites
- Internet Producer/Games and Statistics
- Internet Software Developer
- Internet Systems Specialist-Intern/Co-Op
- Intranet Developer/Programmer
- Lead Programmer
- MacIntosh/PC Technician
- Manager of Interactive Technology
- Manager of Technical Operations and Help Desk
- Network Analysts
- Network/Broadband Manager
- On-line Editor
- Oracle Database Administrator
- Producer
- Production Systems Supervisor
- Programmer Analyst
- Programmer/Database Analyst
- Senior Applications Developer
- Senior Applications Specialist
- Senior CISCO WAN/LAN Analyst
- Senior Internet Producer/Personal Finance
- Senior Network Analyst
- Senior Project Manager—QA
- Senior Quality Assurance Analyst
- Senior Systems Analyst/Client Systems
- Senior Technology Architect
- Senior Technology Architect—Data Systems
- Senior Technology Architect—Production Systems
- Senior UNIX Administrator
- Systems Administrator—AIX
- Systems Analyst/CIS
- Systems Analyst/Manifest

- Systems Engineer
- Systems Support
- Technical Operations Specialist
- Technical Producer
- Technician
- Technology Architect
- Training Coordinator
- UNIX Administrator
- Video Producer
- Web Artist
- Web Producer

4

Show Me the Money!

By now you are probably beginning to wonder what kind of money you should expect to be making if you decide to take a job in the field of information technology. Of course how much money you have the potential to make is a very important factor to consider when deciding on a career. So let us now take a look at the annual salary expectations for people working in various areas of the field.

UNEQUAL PAY FOR EQUAL WORK

Unfortunately, women are still earning less money in this field than their male counterparts. Regardless of the fact that a woman may have the same educational background, be the same age, have equal work experience, and be working at the same job level as a man in the same field, she will likely make less money anyway. As you might have suspected, this female to male salary discrepancy is not seen solely in the field of computers and information technology. But since this is the field we are discussing, we will not go into general equal pay for equal work issues. However, it is significant for you to understand that this discrimination is not exclusive to this field. One positive thing to make note of at this point is that because of the constantly growing nature of the field, there is a consequent need for more people to fill the new jobs. More women are entering the field and more of these women are moving up within their companies and taking higher level jobs with higher salaries.

INCREASE YOUR ANNUAL SALARY

Later on you will read job descriptions by professionals in the various fields of information technology in chapters 5 through 11. You will notice that many of these people were able to increase their annual salaries by moving up as far as they could go within a company and then changing jobs. Another way to increase your earning potential is to become an expert in a particular area. A specialist with expertise in an area of high demand is in a great position, as it now becomes possible for that person to negotiate with potential employers for a desired annual salary. The expert may be able to negotiate an annual salary that is between 3 and 15 percent higher than his or her current annual salary. This, by the way, is the concept of supply and demand.

INDUSTRY FACTORS

How much money you are able to make in any given position will also depend heavily on a number of other factors, such as the size of the company, the actual industry for which you work, and the part of the country in which you happen to be located. All of these things should be taken into consideration when you are searching for your job. Perhaps you will not want to work for a small company because the growth and earning potential will not meet your needs. Or you may decide to move to another part of the country where your particular field of expertise is more in demand and jobs pay better. These are some of the things you will want to think about when the time comes.

The College Placement Council (CPC) is an organization that keeps track of the salaries offered to recent college graduates every year. Within the last five years, the average entry-level annual salary for recent graduates in select areas of information technology are as follows:

Position	Average Salary
Management Information Systems	$30,692
Information Technology	$31,448
Computer Programming	$28,033
Systems Analysis	$33,218

And for those graduating with a master's degree:

Position	Average Salary
MIS	$45,700
Computer Science	$39,786

As previously mentioned, the annual salaries for each subspecialty can range a great deal, depending on the size of the company. The following approximate annual salary ranges are for positions in companies that themselves range from less-than-$50-million companies to over-$1-billion companies. For example, the CIO/VP (chief information officer/vice president) of a company can expect to make anywhere from $94,000 to $130,600 a year, depending on the size of the company he or she is employed by. The rest of this sample is based on the same model.

Position	Salary Range
Director	$65,650 – $89,500
Manager/Supervisor	$52,900 – $64,850
Applications Designer	$48,500 – $53,250
Project Manager	$52,640 – $58,400
Systems Analyst	$38,400 – $43,400
Network Manager (LAN/WAN)	$45,000 – $54,000
Help Desk Manager	$37,000 – $50,000
Technical Support Analyst	$34,500 – $39,500
PC Technician	$29,000 – $35,500
Data Entry Clerk	$19,500 – $22,500

These annual salary ranges also depend on the part of the country you happen to be living and working in.

COST OF LIVING

Your annual salary will depend on where you live and work because different parts of the country have different costs of living. The cost of living is the actual amount of money that it costs to live in a certain area, based on how much the things in that area cost. Employees in all industries have to be paid accordingly. So you may find that you will be able to make more money living in Chicago than you will make if you live in Peoria. However, you will also need more money to live on if you live in Chicago than if you live in Peoria. You must take cost of living differences into consideration when deciding where to work.

BENEFITS PACKAGES

When you are considering accepting a job with a particular company, you should take into consideration more than just the actual annual salary you will be earning. There are other factors and benefits, in addition to your annual salary, that determine whether or not you are being properly compensated for the work you are doing. You need to consider the entire benefits package when you are considering what you are worth in the industry. What else does the company have to offer you, in addition to your annual salary? Benefits you can look for in a good job are health insurance, dental insurance, and life insurance. Disability pay, vacation pay, sick leave, and paid holidays should also be included. The promise of an end of the year bonus, a pension plan, a profit-sharing plan, and employee stock ownership or purchase plans are all added benefits that you can look for, although you should not expect all companies to offer these benefits. As you enter the job market, do your homework and find out all you can about any company you are interested in working for even before you go in for your interview. Then, when you do go in for the interview, ask as many important questions as you feel the need to have answers for.

THE BOTTOM LINE ON ANNUAL SALARY

If you choose to pursue a career in information technology, you can expect to be able to earn an attractive annual salary. Qualified professionals are attracted to this field not only because of the excellent annual salary potential but also by the benefits packages most companies offer, training programs, continuing education opportunities, ever changing job responsibilities, the potential to grow as the industry grows, and the forecast that the industry will continue to grow and require more professionals to fill positions, thus offering a certain degree of job security. These are all reasons why people like you are choosing to pursue careers in information technology every day. The bottom line when it comes to annual salary is that you will be paid for what you bring to the company and how well you do your job. Know what you and your skills, knowledge, and expertise are worth before you accept a job. Remember that there is still a certain degree of variation from company to company and from state to state. To find out more about annual salaries within the industry, write to:

Robert Half International, Inc.
P.O. Box 33597
Kansas City, MO 64120

This company is one of the largest recruiting firms of professionals in the information industry and therefore has a great deal of information about the professional aspects of the field, annual salaries included.

5

Wade Brown, Internet Specialist

The next group of chapters includes interviews with one or more information technology professionals. These professionals have spoken candidly about their careers in information technology, giving details about how they found their way into the field, what positions they now hold, and what they did to get there. Their stories are meant to give you a general idea of what it is like to work in various areas of this broad field we call information technology. These people represent a population of workers from recent college graduates to twenty-plus-year veterans in the field. Their experiences range from the first day on a new job to the last week before retirement. Their educational backgrounds span the range from some college education to master's degree program graduates. The ages of these particular professionals represent a range from early 20s to mid-50s. Some of their names have been changed to protect their privacy, but they are without a doubt all real people. Read all of these chapters or just read the ones that match the areas of information technology that interest you the most. Either way, you will get a general sampling of what it is like to work in various areas of the field of information technology.

Our first subject is Wade Brown, a network, personal computer, information technology, and Internet specialist at an Internet/Extranet development company in California. Wade talks about what it takes to do his job.

I work for an Internet/Extranet development company in California. What I do is write the programs that allow people to share information across the World Wide Web. For example, our programs allow a particular company to have offices in different states, or even in different countries, and share data (information) privately so that people who do not work for the company are not able to see it. The Internet is a very cost-effective way to send information, but in general it is not a very private way. This is where my job comes in. In order to get privacy on the Internet, the companies need some help from people like me. For instance, if someone wanted to buy a book from an on-line bookstore, they might want to use their credit card, but they would not want anyone else to be able to see what the credit card number is. I set up the privacy that only allows the on-line bookstore to see the credit card number. Basically I write code (what programs are written in), and troubleshoot network problems. Computers "talk" to each other to share information, and when two or more computers can "talk" to each other, it is called a network. The Internet is the largest network of computers today.

I started working with computers when I was in high school. In fact, computers were my first job. I started out earning $4.47 an hour in 1985, which was just over minimum wage. That first job I had was a job where I filed data. It was like arranging files in a file cabinet, but on a computer. The same way a well-organized file cabinet makes files easy to find, a well-organized database makes data easy to find. Since high school, I have worked at other places, but I think I am happiest when I am working with computers. Computers "think," or *process data, in a certain kind of way. It is all very logical. I think that way, too, so computers and I are a good match. Besides, I like to help people get the information they need to build things, or buy things, or just talk to each other.*

Computers are changing all the time. Every year there are new computers and new ways to use them. Anyone who is thinking about working with computers should know that there is always a lot to learn and new things to learn every day. I even take home books to learn at home, just like homework. Today I am earning $45,000 a year, and I expect to see that grow to $60,000 or $75,000 or more in the next couple of years.

I do not think I will be leaving the field of computers and information technology anytime soon. Information technology is all around us, even if we do not always notice. When you go to a store with a POS (point of sale) system and buy a pack of gum, for example, the checker uses a scanner to scan the barcode on the item as you check out. The scanner "tells" the cash register what item is being purchased. The cash register "tells" the store computer that there is one less pack of gum on the shelf. The store computer then knows when to "tell" the computer at the warehouse that the store needs to have more gum sent out. You see … information technology really is everywhere. It really is!

6

Matt Helms, Desktop Support Supervisor

Matt Helms provides support to all employees who work at computers at an educational toy manufacturer in an Illinois town. As the desktop support supervisor for the company, he is a manager in charge of two employees and he is responsible for all computer equipment outside of the server room. Relatively new to the field, Matt easily recalls what he did to land his job.

I graduated from college with certifications to teach junior high and high school English and social studies. I did some at-home instruction for a child who had been kicked out of his junior high school for bringing a gun to school. I also did some substituting in high schools. However, after several years of failing to land a permanent teaching job, I decided to look around for something else to do. I had a few office jobs, mostly clerical and temporary work. For two years before I starting working at my current position, I sold Christmas decorations to retail chains. Other than that, I tried acting (some community theater) and played guitar and sang in a few punk bands that went absolutely nowhere. I really was not sure what I wanted to do, so I tried it all!

Finally, I ended up in the field of information science. Getting into the support area of information science just seemed to be a natural extension of my teaching training. Instead of doing normal things like dating during high school, I had a computer. It was an Atari 800XL, which was a pretty close equivalent to the old Atari game system that almost every kid had in the late 1970s and early 1980s. For my own amusement, I programmed a lot of games on that machine. When I went to college my social life finally picked up and I left the computer behind and concentrated on music instead. When I had that Christmas decoration sales job, I was the office computer support person by default. This was because I was the only one who had really used a computer before and I was willing to dig in and try to figure out the company's computers. Eventually, I began to realize that working on computers and helping people with their problems satisfied me much more than arguing with people about Christmas lights!

I was hired as a desktop support specialist, which is an hourly position. I was an employee at the bottom of the employee totem pole. However, even at that hourly wage I was making 13 percent more than what I had been bringing in when I worked in sales. A month later, I was promoted to network system specialist. My duties remained primarily unchanged, although there was a little more involvement in the server room for me. I was now being paid a straight annual salary and I got a 6 percent raise. At the time we were trying to have everyone in my department know a little bit of everything. Nine months after I was hired, I was promoted to lead desktop support and given a 10 percent raise to compensate for the new duties. These new duties put me in charge of troubleshooting, maintaining, and upgrading every piece of computer equipment in the entire office. A second support person was also hired to help me out. His position is desktop support specialist. Finally, just after I had marked one year in the information science field, I was promoted again, this time to the position called desktop support supervisor, and I was given management responsibilities over what is now a subdepartment of our MIS department. I received another 10 percent raise with this promotion. I was also allowed to hire two more employees and I may be looking into hiring a few more people sometime down the road.

I think I have had a fast rise in this career just at this one job, but I may have reached a high-water mark for a while. I am definitely more interested in the user support side of information science rather than the straight technical work, so I imagine I will never lose that part of my job. I see myself pretty much always working as a support supervisor. I do not think I could get into consulting because I believe in building a relationship with a company and sticking to it as much as possible.

Basically I have no specific educational background to support my job skills. I am all self-taught. I have taken some two-day or week-long classes since I started working in my current position. I feel that because information science is such a rapidly changing and hands-on field, it can be somewhat difficult to get good specific training. I think you have to constantly try out new things within your system, read books and periodicals, and take classes to keep up-to-date with all of the rapid advances in the field.

7

John Hutton, Senior Consultant, and Denise Pagel, Web Administrator

John Hutton is a senior consultant at a leading provider of e-business solutions for fast-growing and middle-market companies. Just a few years out of school, John has already found success and job satisfaction.

As senior consultant, I do Lotus Notes/ Domino/Internet application development. I have been working in the field of information science for two and a half years now. Before I got into information science, I went to college. I attended Miami University in Oxford, Ohio, and earned a bachelor of science degree in accountancy and management information science. I am also a principal certified Lotus professional in application development R4 and a principal certified Lotus professional in application development R5.

I love this field of work. It is always changing! Especially when you are in consulting, as I am. I do not do the same thing every day, and I love that. I may learn something from working with one client that I might be able to apply to another client's project.

I started out as a junior level developer right out of college. College courses usually teach only the basics of information science, so most employers usually send junior level people out to get specific training. In my case I went to Lotus Notes training. The harder you work and develop your skills, the more you really enjoy your work, and the faster you are promoted and move up the ladder. It is a win-win situation in this field, as far as I am concerned.

Starting annual salary in this particular area is around the mid-30s, with full benefits. The company I work for is generous with its opportunities for overtime and bonuses. Some companies also offer stock options. Each company handles compensation differently.

Two years later, I have been promoted to senior consultant with a complementary annual salary. As I move up the ladder in this fast-developing field, I am given more responsibilities. This is getting me ready for a management position. That is where I see myself progressing to in the future.

DENISE PAGEL

Denise Pagel is the Web administrator for a software company in a suburb of Chicago that is a reseller of computer software and add-on hardware (memory, modems, etc.) to business users. She is an eleven-year veteran at her company.

I am one-third of the team that works on my company's Intranet site. The first person on our team works in our systems department and is responsible for the back-end Web server. The second person, our Web developer, is responsible for determining the additional functions our Web site will offer to our customers. I am responsible for the day-to-day maintenance of the site. I prepare the text developed by different departments, such as marketing and human resources, and place all of the content that our customers see on the Web site itself. In terms of in-house information systems, the company I work for does not have a single repository for companywide information. We are still small enough that we can get away with that. We have Lotus Notes for general items (the human resource manual, phone lists, and such) and we have a computer application for our customer and transaction information. Records at the office are kept for two years on-line. Older information is put onto backup tapes and not accessed.

I have been with the company for eleven years, changing positions as the company grew. When I joined my company, there were only twenty other employees. I began in the accounts receivable department, posting payments to customers' accounts. As the company grew, my position continually shifted. I would retain some of the duties of my previous position as I began each new position. I have been in the accounts receivable, purchasing, inventory control, accounts payable, desktop publishing, and marketing areas of my company over the last eleven years, with my duties changing every eighteen to twenty-four months. It has kept the work fresh since some aspect of the job is always new. I took over the desktop publishing area in 1995, before the Internet was readily available. We offered a fax-back service at that time. As the Internet replaced the fax as a means of contacting customers with product information, I took classes and my position transitioned from desktop publisher to Webmaster. Our first Web site went live in the spring of 1997, and the fax service was dropped eight months later.

I have always felt that my greatest asset is my ability to adapt to the changing needs of my company. This is a big part of having a career in information science, as the field is constantly changing. My ability to adapt was never more important than it is right now, with the fluid nature of the Web.

I got into information science somewhat by accident. It was my interest in another area that pushed me toward information science. I have always had a love of history. By trying to understand how different viewpoints affected the final outcome of some event, I learned how to research. When you do research, you collect a great many disparate pieces of information that have to be sorted in some fashion so that you can find the piece of information you are looking for. I discovered I had a knack for information management.

Businesses generate a great deal of information each year—the products they manufacture, the customers they sell to, the invoices for those sales, payment information, and so forth. In the old days, all of this information was on paper and people were hired to do nothing else but file that paper away so that it could be located again when it was needed. That is the kind of mindless drudge work that computers are designed to eliminate. *Most businesses live with one foot in the computer technology world and the other foot still holding down a pile of paper, however. So far, there is not one single "good answer" on how businesses should store and retrieve this information. In its broadest sense, information technology considers all the ways data can be created, stored, and retrieved.*

I had originally intended to get a master of science degree in library science, but I discovered in graduate school that it was better to have practical library experience before attempting to get the degree. My actual undergraduate major was anthropology and my minor was history, although I actually had enough hours in history for a double major if that had been allowed when I was in school. While the subject matter I studied may have prepared me for dealing with office politics rather than business practices, I also developed the ability to adapt to changing conditions. I learned to view a process in its entirety, break it into smaller segments, and then streamline the process. That is basically the same as the total quality management principle that many businesses are now adopting.

This branch of information science has a fairly competitive annual salary. The company I work for stays up-to-date concerning the industry standard pay scale. Our human resources department reviews the reference materials available providing job descriptions and their annual salary ranges in the Midwest. Our annual salary range is adjusted to remain within the standard for our job position. The plus side to this arrangement is that we are generally assured of a raise *each year. The negative side is that, in effect, we have a cap on the maximum annual salary we can earn. My current position is rated as between $25,000 to $35,000 per year. However, anything involving the Web is in a state of constant change and the annual salary range for Web professionals runs from $20,000 for an entry-level person who simply pastes text onto a page to $125,000 for a Web developer. Unlike many other companies, we have nonsalary items that add to the attractiveness of the job. A flexible time-off policy, tuition assistance, a company matching contribution to our 401K accounts, a company sponsored trip for employees in recognition of each five years of service, and a paid month sabbatical for employees in recognition of each seven years of service all add significantly to the morale of the workplace. So I find that in addition to my basic job satisfaction, I am given a great number of perks that keep me even happier with the field of work I have chosen as my career. All companies are not necessarily as generous as the one that I work for, but many companies have great benefits and perks. If you enjoy what you do, these extras are really just a nice bonus.*

The introduction of the Internet has changed business just as completely as the telephone changed business 100 years ago. We are still in the "Wild West" phase of that transition. All kinds of business ideas will be tried over the next few years. I do not know exactly where I see myself in the next five, ten, or fifteen years. I really do find this field to be quite fascinating and so I predict I will continue to find new and exciting things to work on as the company and the field itself keep growing.

8

Julia James, Web Coordinator, and Samantha Hoffman, Transfer Coordinator and Data Mapper

Julia James works for an Illinois-based educational toy company. Although she did not start out aiming for a career in information technology, her background helped her to attain an interesting job in the field.

> *I am the Web coordinator for an educational toy company. I am responsible for coordinating the content of the company's Web site, creating pages, maintaining databases, and making sure our e-commerce is running smoothly. I have been at my current job since October 1998, but I have actually been doing similar work since about 1996. I never had any idea that I would end up working in information technology. I graduated with a bachelor's degree in fine arts with an emphasis in graphic design. After college I worked for an association for life insurance agents in their audio/visual department. I created slides for speakers and I also created videos. After a while I got involved in developing their first Web site and that is where I was introduced to the field of information technology. After that job, I worked briefly for an outsourcing company developing other companies' Web sites, and then I came to the educational toy company where I am now employed.*

I really like what I am doing right now. However, in terms of annual salary, I feel that if I had had more of a computer background coming into the field, my current annual salary would be higher. Nonetheless, I think I will stay in this field indefinitely. I think the Web is constantly changing, so it is important to keep up with what is happening in the industry. That is what makes this career so interesting—every day is different and new and better technology is constantly being invented or created and then introduced. It is very exciting to think about what could be coming next.

As you can see, the field of information technology is not just a male-dominated career field. With all the different jobs that fall under the general heading of information technology, there are just as many enjoyable jobs for women as there are for men. None of the jobs within the field are specifically identified with one gender or the other. It is really just a matter of personal preference and what you as an individual find interesting and challenging as a career choice.

SAMANTHA HOFFMAN

Samantha Hoffman is another woman who has taken her experience and expertise and made a career for herself in the field of information technology.

I work for a mortgage company as their transfer coordinator and data mapper. I have been at my current company since 1994. Before I came to this job, I did a really wide variety of different things. I was a travel consultant for a while, I had a job as a receptionist, I managed a Blockbuster Video store, and once

I even worked in a tollbooth for a stretch. I was kind of thrown into the field of information technology, but mostly it was the opportunity to make a decent living that attracted me to the field in general. I had some college education and training, but most of the experience I brought to my job was all field and work-related experience—you know, things I had learned on the job while working at some of my other jobs. Also, my parents work in the field of computers, so I was exposed to it at home from an early age. Since I lacked some of the more formal educational requirements for this field, I started out in an entry-level position at my current place of employment.

As I gained experience and learned new skills, I was eventually able to move up the ladder within the company by showing what good work I could produce. It was relatively easy for me, actually. I enjoy what I do and I learn things rather quickly, so doing good work and moving up seemed to come as quite natural steps, I think. Because I have moved so vertically within the company, my annual salary has been greatly affected. Since 1994 when I started, I have received over a 111 percent increase in my annual salary. I was really glad to find out that I was right about the financial opportunities available within this field.

9

Michael Jaltuch, Information Science Specialist, and Ed Kuehl, Information Technology Manager

Michael Jaltuch is an information science specialist who grew up with a family background in the industry, which helped to bring him to his current position.

I work for an e-business company in the information science industry. E-business is short for electronic business. I am an information science specialist and project manager. I have been doing this job for two and a half years, basically since I graduated from college. Before I worked at this job, I had several part-time jobs while I was in college.

I actually knew from an early age that this was what I wanted to do with my future. As I got older and learned more about computers and information science, I realized that this is where the world is going. I also liked the fact that this is a field that is continually changing, which makes the job I do very exciting. It is definitely never boring.

My educational background is actually in the field of communications. I did not major in the field of information science. However, I have always been drawn to it. When I first started working in the field, I had an entry-level position called Help Desk. After a while I moved up from that point. Actually, I have been promoted quite a bit in the mere two and a half years that I have been employed in the field. With my promotions, my annual salary has increased dramatically. In fact, it has almost doubled since I first started working.

I see myself continuing to learn about the field of information science. I would like to become a certified project manager and then continue to educate myself from a technical standpoint. I would like to be someone who not only runs a project but knows all the ins and outs of the project as well. I know I will stay in this field for a long time.

Ed Kuehl

As a fifteen-year veteran of information technology work, Ed Kuehl shares the story of how he was first inspired to work with computers and how far building on a little bit of curiosity was able to take him.

I just started a new job today! I am working at a manufacturing company again, which is the same kind of job I just left. The new company has both an office side and a factory side. My position is information technology manager. I am responsible for providing the support for both sides of the company (the office and the factory). Actually, I am responsible for all aspects of the computer systems and the networking. The network, of course, is all of the computers connecting together so we can share data, access the Internet, and send e-mail within the company and also outside of the company.

My responsibilities also include all of the company's phone systems, including the cellular phones and the pagers. Basically, anything and everything that has to do with communications falls under my job title.

Indirectly, I have been working in the field of information science since roughly 1985. What I mean by "indirectly" is that information science had been part of my job responsibility for some time before it became my only responsibility. At the first company I worked for, back in the mid-1980s, I was the purchasing manager. This was really before computers were very widely used. The company I was working for at the time finally got a computer to do small bits of work. It became part of my job then to do that work. It was a small company, and my job description was still rather broad at the time. After seeing what we could do with the one computer, which I mainly used for purchasing, I convinced the company to get a few more computers so we could expand the work that we could do with them.

In 1988, I moved to another company. It was there that my interest in computers was really piqued. So in 1989, I enrolled in Northern Illinois University's graduate program. I started to work on my master's degree in computers in 1989. I finally earned my master of science degree in management information systems in 1994. Consequently, my job description changed after that, and I have been working just in information systems since about 1995 or 1996.

Before I got into information systems full-time, I did a little of everything. At one time or another, my job title was manager of inside sales, operations manager, office manager, purchasing manager, and information tech-nologies manager. Basically I went from a small branch of a company with a general job description to a larger plant (owned by the same company) with more specific job responsibilities. To be honest, having all of these jobs under my belt really helps me a lot now because I am familiar with many different aspects of the field, and I know what other parts of the business need from me as the manager of information science.

I first came into contact with computers and the field of information science when I was in the navy. I was on a submarine for six years during the Vietnam era. That was the 1970s. While I was aboard ship, IBM introduced the personal computer. The computer had to be kept in a safe place. Since I was the person put in charge of the computer, I got my very own little office to keep it safe. It was just me and my computer. I had a lot of time to play around with that computer. Mostly I played games. There was one that I particularly liked. It was a Star Trek *game. That is really where my inter-est in computers came from. The rest of it just seemed to naturally follow.*

Before I got my master's degree, I already had an undergraduate degree, which the United States actu-ally funded because I was in the navy. I had a double major in finance (which I thought I would need to get along in the business world) and management. I went back to school for my master's degree in information science when I realized just how much I really liked the work I was doing. I knew I would want to continue in the field and move up the ladder. To do that, I realized, I would first need to further my education.

I never actually held an entry-level job in any computer department. I was responsible for computers on a small scale for quite a while. Earning my master's degree moved me right up to a manager position. So basically I just skipped over all of the lower level positions. Most people, however, typically start in entry-level positions and then move up in the company as they acquire more and more skills and learn new things. For example, in his or her first position, someone might be responsible for maintaining the office's PCs as a technician. Then he or she might advance to the position of systems administrator for the servers, then become the network specialists, working with the networks, routers, and LANs. Then he or she might advance to become the information technologies manager. But I personally skipped all of those intermediate steps because of the companies at which I was employed, and then because I got my master's degree.

When I was promoted from my original position to that of information technologies manager, I earned a $10,000 raise. When I accepted the job that I just started today, I got another comparable raise. So overall, since I first started, my annual salary has increased over $20,000.

When I think about my future in the field of information science, I see the potential to continue to advance until I become the CIO (chief information officer). That would be the next step for me. However, this probably will not happen at the company I am now working for because it is too small. I will have to go to a larger company if I want to pursue the CIO position. You see, not all companies even have a CIO position.

If I were to stay at this company let us just say "forever," my position would remain director or information technologies manager. If I had stayed at my previous place of employment, I would have advanced to become the director of information technologies. The information technologies managers at our different plants would all have been reporting to the one director of information technologies, which would have been me. This specific structure actually varies somewhat from company to company, however, depending a great deal on both the size and the needs of the individual company.

Another aspect of information science that is becoming more and more important on an almost daily basis is, of course, the Internet. All aspects of the Internet—programming, e-commerce, building Web pages—are booming. It is really another aspect of the field, aside from the area that I work in, that you can really get into and know that you will have a strong future and great upward mobility.

10

Adam Frederickson, Video Game Designer, and Barbara Radomsky, Small Business Owner

Adam Frederickson worked in several different aspects of the information science industry before finally deciding to incorporate and start his very own business right out of his basement.

I own my own company. My company makes coin-operated video games. I prefer to go by the job title of chief engineer but I am also the CEO (chief executive officer) of the company. I got into this industry (video games) back in 1989. Before games, I worked for a large film company for about a year and a half. It was a drag, so I quit and hooked up with a friend of mine from college who was starting up a game company.

Information science is really just one part of my job. These days, it is important to know everything about computers, including how to set up and maintain networks. I need to know many information science–related concepts in order to do my job. I create and maintain an office network that consists of several computers: one in

Win95 and the rest are Linux. All of the computers in the network need to talk to each other and to the Internet. I also provide an "Internet presence" for the company. I maintain my company's Web site so that others can see what the company does and consider hiring me to do their work. I also set up a system to sell my company's products over the Internet. Another really important part of my job is making all of the computers secure from hackers.

I actually have a bachelor of science degree in electrical engineering. I guess you can say I have sort of been all over the place in terms of the directions I have taken, career-wise. I started out designing electronics (hardware). Then I learned how to program, which took me a fairly long time to get good at. Eventually, maybe about a year ago now, I started up my own company. So far I am the only company employee. However, I do occasionally work with a few guys who are independent contractors. My annual salary has grown slowly over the course of my career, but it has always been heavily incentive-based. If I made a product that made money, I got a piece of the action. Now, as a business owner, I really make very little money unless I can make a profitable product. But the upside is much greater. If things work out, I get to be the one with the potential to get rich, rather than making the money for someone else. I have never liked having a boss telling me what to do. Owning my own business gives me flexibility, plus I get to be my own boss. Thus far I am really enjoying being self-employed. Up until about three months ago, I worked in a very small home office (120 square feet). That was a sufficient amount of space for a while because all I really needed to do was sit and write programs. Now I am at a more advanced stage where I work on big prototypes and have artists and visitors around regularly. So I moved into a small office (about 450 square feet) five miles from my home. So far this has been working out great. Soon, I will probably hire an artist to work with me in the office on a full-time basis. Since I have the office space now I am ready for that— there is enough room. The other reason I felt I needed an office outside of my home is that I am the father of three children, ages one, four, and five, so you can imagine that things could be a bit distracting at home.

My strongest recommendation to anyone considering entering the field of information science is to learn how to program in C. I also tell everybody to learn the operating system Linux. It is free. It works great. It is incredible at networking. All source code is free and open.

The information science field is already huge and it looks like it will continue to grow for a long time. Making games is very hard work, and I would not necessarily recommend the industry to most people. But if you enjoy hard work and you have a creative streak, then I would definitely tell you to go for it.

BARBARA RADOMSKY

Barbara Radomsky worked in the field of computers and information technology for many years before deciding to start her own business so she could stay home and raise her children. It seemed like a logical decision to Barbara.

I have always loved logic, and working with computers involves a lot of logic. That is where my original

81

interest in the field comes from. So I earned a degree in computer science and have taken a number of more specific courses since I qualified. I have been working in computers and the field of information science for more than twenty years. In fact, I have been working in the industry since I graduated from college. Now I am the manager of my own computer consulting company. I was a computer programmer and then a consultant with other companies before I decided to start my own company six years ago. My company develops computer systems for small companies and nonprofit organizations. My main responsibilities include investigating my clients' needs, designing and programming computer solutions for them, and training their employees to use the systems.

Twenty-two years ago, I began working as a programmer for a large mining company. I was promoted to programmer-analyst during the three years that I was there. My next job was in the computer consulting division of a big accounting firm. I researched computer packages and gave our clients advice on which computers and computer packages to buy. I earned about 25 percent more at that company than I did in my previous job. But I left the accounting firm after only two years because I wanted to develop the systems myself and not just look at systems that other people had written.

I joined a company that specializes in computer systems development for large companies. I worked there for twelve years. During that time, my annual salary increased by over 150 percent. I went from being a programmer-analyst to being a project manager, responsible for up to eight people on my team.

I left this last job when my first child was born. That is when I went into business for myself. Now I work part-time out of my home. In some years my net income exceeds the annual salary I received in my last full-time job, but in other years it is substantially less. That is just the way working for yourself can be.

I love working in information science and with computers. I also enjoy being able to use my skills to assist the nonprofit community as well. I got involved with working with nonprofit companies when my first client wanted work done, but could not find an established company to do it for them at a reasonable charge. A friend of mine who worked for one of the established companies called me and told me of the situation. I liked the fact that I could give the nonprofit company a great system at a reasonable price. At the same time, I benefited because I would not have been paid as much for the work had I done it while working for someone else.

This has proven to be a terrific and satisfying career for me, so I plan to continue to work within this field. I will also continue to work for myself, as I love being able to choose the hours that I want to work. This gives me the flexibility to spend time with my family. This is a really enjoyable job, especially if you are intrigued by logic and you like working with people.

11

Jay Leib, Director of Software Sales and Training, and Nagesh Reddy, Senior Consultant

Jay Leib has found a niche within the industry of information science that capitalizes on his sales experience and expertise while also allowing him to work with computers, which has always been one of his hobbies.

For the past four years I have been working for a company that provides litigation support services technology to law firms and to the legal market in general. I am the director of software sales and training. What this means is that I supply, sell, and support the technology that applies to what lawyers do. Then I set up training sessions and I go in and train the law firms to use the technology. In layman's terms, I help lawyers use technology to expedite how they practice law. I set up databases and computer software for their evidence and discovery materials, and I set up real-time computers for live feeds for court reporters. I also set up and sell hardware, or electronic storage centers, for the law firms to use when they have large amounts of documentation that need to be filed and stored. I do quite a bit of traveling in my position. In fact, last month alone I was out of town on business trips more than I was home. I was beginning to wonder why I was paying rent for a place I was never home to enjoy. But to tell you the truth, I do not really mind traveling. In the evenings when I am on a business trip, I often get to see a little bit of the cities I have traveled to. It is not like being on a vacation, but it does provide me with a welcome change of scenery now and then.

I was actually in an artistic field in college. I majored in television and video at Columbia College in Chicago. However, since I graduated from college just a few years ago, the jobs I have had have all been in sales. Always for fun, though, I liked to set up computer systems for my friends and relatives. I still enjoy doing this and in fact I recently set up a really neat Web site for my niece and nephews. I surprised them with it over the holidays. I got into the information technology part of sales because I realized that technology is affecting the way that all businesses are run these days, from the way doctors practice medicine to the way lawyers practice law, and so on. I wanted to be a part of it all in some capacity. On my own I have taken a lot of certification classes and courses in technology and related technical fields like networking and software. That helps me sell my product because it gives me a better understanding of what I am dealing with. It helps me to better answer my clients' questions, as well. Technology is always evolving and it impacts everything. I want to continue to evolve my skills right along with the evolution of the field.

A person joining our company at an entry-level position right now could expect to earn an annual salary of about $30,000. In my position now, I am

85

earning an annual salary at the six-figure mark. There is great earning potential in this field, obviously.

In the field of information technology there is always something new and exciting on the horizon. I like that. I like not knowing exactly what will be coming up next, yet knowing that I have put myself in a position to be a part of whatever it is. That really excites me!

NAGESH REDDY

Nagesh moved from his native country, India, several years ago to pursue a dream in the field of computers and information technology. It was a tough road for Nagesh to get where he is now. Education, hard work, and persistence have paid off.

I am currently employed by a professional services company that deals with taxes, auditing, management consulting, change leadership, software consulting, and things like that. There are several divisions within my company. One of them is the consulting group. Within the consulting group there are several groups that specialize in different areas of information systems. I work for the consulting group with the EAI (enterprise applications and integration) group as a senior consultant. Think of it like this: parent, the main company; division, the consulting group; subdivision or specialization group, enterprise applications and integration (EAI).

I have been doing this kind of work for a total of eight years, but I have only been with this consulting group for two years. Before I started work, I was studying! I have a bachelor's degree in computer science, engineering, and technology. My main attraction to the field of information science was . . . money! Just kidding. I always wanted to be different and do what not many people have done before. In 1985, when I was still in school, this was a brand new field in India. As I heard more about it, I became more interested in it, and then I decided that this is what I wanted to do: design and manage corporate information (data and systems). To have the power and ability to make or break a corporation in a sense. I mean that in a purely joking way, but it really does illustrate how much power I actually have in my position. What I really wanted to do was help corporations manage their information effectively, thereby improving productivity and profits.

In addition to my bachelor's degree in computer science, engineering, and technology from Bangalore University in India, I decided a few years ago to further my education. I am now halfway through my work toward a master's degree in software engineering.

Eight years ago, I started working as a trainee. If you can believe this, I was not getting paid at all for the first three months! And after that I was getting only about $30 a month. This money was not like an actual salary but more for expenses. Luckily, I was not totally dependent on this money for my living. I have a wonderful family who supported me all the way through college until I got a decent job and was able to support myself completely. I did this for another three months and then I joined another company. I worked with the new company for two years. By the time I left them, I was a software engineer getting about $200 a month.

Then I moved to another country and joined a company as software engineer with a starting salary of about $1,400 a month, which came to about $16,800 a year. When I left this company after two years I was getting about $2,000 a month, roughly $24,000 a year. I came to the United States in 1996, and my salary has been increasing yearly since then. I would rather not disclose the actual figures here, but let me just say that what I am making now is significantly more than I was making even when I first came to this country. One day I would like to start up a company of my own. My company will revolutionize the way we do business and manage information.

I really love what I do. I think that as long as you like this field, as long as you have a passion for it, I would say to any student: "Go for it." Honestly, I think that one of the best things about this industry is that there are several hundred types of jobs available within the information systems industry. Try to find out as much as possible and go for the type of job you like the most.

12

Equal Opportunity Employment and Working from Home

When you stop and think about all the different kinds of jobs people have held in the last 100 years, it is impossible not to see what a relatively young field computers and computer-based information technology is. Today, students are learning about computers and information systems at school from a very early age. The information technology industry is growing by leaps and bounds and the need for qualified professionals in the field is growing right along with it. The best part about this rapid growth is that because companies need qualified professionals and they need them now, they are looking for the best person to do the job, rather than looking to hire a person of a particular race or gender. People of all ages, races, genders, and even some physically-challenged persons are competing for and finding rewarding work in the information technology industry. Managers want the most skilled persons to fill their job openings. If you have what it takes to get the job done, managers will want you.

It is important to note here, however, that employers are still looking to hire the most qualified people overall. These qualifications do include educational background, but also your personal character. In other words, what you are like, how well you conduct yourself in a professional environment, how well you work in a team, how you get along with others in the workplace, and other factors are important. But all things being equal in terms of education, experience, and character, any two people should each have an equal chance for landing a job.

The fields of computers and information technology are actually among the more liberal fields, in terms of equal opportunity employment. Any person can find challenging, lucrative employment in the information technology industry if he or she meets the usual qualifications:

- Good communication skills
- Leadership potential
- Technical experience
- Strong math skills
- Willingness to work hard
- Proper education or comparative work experience
- Good attitude and teamwork skills
- Flexibility and ability to change or shift responsibilities as the field changes
- Ability to learn new things quickly

If you have a physical challenge, you may actually find that information technology, because of its use of computers, is a field in which you may excel. Information technology uses the skills of the mind far more than the skills of the body. Another advantage of this field is that most of the jobs can be done from home, as long as you have a good computer and Internet access. Physically-challenged individuals can perform almost any information technology job as well as any able-bodied person can perform it.

The main thing is that if you have computer skills in information technology, you are employable. There is a job out there just waiting for you, whether you work in an office, out in the field, or from a computer in your living room, which brings us to the next topic: working from home.

HOME AND OFFICE: ONE AND THE SAME

As mentioned in the previous section, many people work from their homes because of a physical disability. Other people work at home because their age or health prevents them from going to an office. In other words, either they have to go to school and are too young to be employed full-time or they are too old or their disability prevents them from getting around easily anymore. These are not the only reasons why an information technology professional might choose to work from home, however. Aside from the obvious reason for working at home—you can stay in your pajamas all day long—some of the reasons why people prefer to work from home instead of in a company's office are listed here:

- To save money on transportation
- To save money on business clothes
- To share child-rearing responsibilities with spouse
- To work at night or at odd hours
- To work more productively by yourself
- To take time off when you need to or want to

Millions of people work full-time or part-time for companies outside of the home. They go to an office during set hours and they bring home a regular paycheck. This is the norm, but plenty of people do not feel that this is the best work situation for them. So instead of following the mainstream way of working, they work from their own home. It takes a lot of discipline and self-motivation to work at home. You will be the one responsible for getting yourself up at a reasonable hour and starting work at a time that allows you to get everything done. There will be no time card to punch. You will be on your own and responsible for yourself. The distractions may be great. Nonetheless, some people really feel that working from home is the way to go.

There are several different ways in which a person can work from home. You can run a small business from your home. You can be employed by an outside company and have a computer-link to the mainframe computer in the company's office. Or you can be an independent contractor or freelancer.

If you run a small business, you are the boss. You may have one or two other employees working with you. It will be up to you to come up with a product and to produce that product. If you work for a company, you will do the same kind of work that you would be doing if you actually went in to the office. You are responsible to a boss. If you are an independent contractor or a freelancer, you will take jobs as they come. You will do work that other companies ask you to do without actually being employed by the companies. Companies hire independent contractors to do the work that they do not have enough staffing or the right staffing to get done.

Financially, your safest at-home work route would be working for another company from home. This will guarantee you your regular paychecks, as if you were still actually working in the office. Freelancing or independent contracting can make you a lot of money or very little money. How much money you can make depends on several factors: how aggressive you are at finding companies to give you work, how many projects you can take on at once, what the market happens to be like at any given time, how much you charge companies for the work that you do, and so on. You may have a really good month followed by a really dry month. You take a lot of chances becoming an independent contractor. Owning your own business can be even more risky, however. You may have to purchase additional office equipment for your employees as well as insurance for having these people working in your home. You will have to pay them, as well. There will be a lot of demands on the income of the company and paying yourself will come last. This does not mean that you cannot make money owning your own business. In fact, many large companies of today started out as someone's small business. Any work-at-home venture takes a lot of hard work and dedication. But in the end, the rewards can be great. About half of all the people who work at home are women. People in all sorts of professions work from home. Information service jobs make up a large portion of the work done from home across the country. The opportunities for working comfortably and successfully from home are abundant. To start out you will need little more than your personal computer and some software, a link to the Internet and e-mail, and a comfy chair.

People work from home for so many different reasons. Some people work from home because they were not happy working for outside companies or were tired of office politics. Some people prefer to stay home so as to save money on child care and actually get to spend time with their children. Other people start up as independent contractors either because they are having trouble finding a job or because they were laid off from a job. Sometimes a person has to move to another area to follow a spouse to a new job and rather than finding a new job, the person stays with his or her company but switches to doing the work from home. If you think you might want to work from home, talk to some people who are already working from home. Find out whether there is an at-home market for your information technology specialty. You may want to gain some experience out in the workforce before you take your work home with you.

I woke up one morning and decided that this would be a cool thing to do. Really. I was too naive to let the potential obstacles bother me. If I had not been single and relatively commitment-free, or if I had had an inkling of just how difficult it can be to be successful starting a new information technology company, I might never have done it; thank heavens for youthful exuberance (and inexperience)!

—Michael Radomsky, executive vice president

13

A Final Word

Job opportunities in the field of information technology are abundant. Just check out your local newspaper's Sunday job section. The future of employment opportunities in information technology and related computer fields is promising. As areas of need change, you may change your specialization, or at least be willing to branch out to different areas and learn new things. But you already know that the world of computers and information technology has been growing by leaps and bounds in recent years.

Right now the highest demand in information technology is in two general areas: The high-level executives are a much-needed group, as are the fresh-out-of-school entry-level applicants who have knowledge of the newest technologies. Over the next ten years, jobs in a number of fields are expected to be the highest in demand. Among these are computer operations researcher, computer engineer, data processing equipment repair specialist, and systems analyst. As the industry as a whole continues its rapid growth, the job opportunities will continue to grow as well. By the year 2005, computer and data processing services are expected to create almost 800,000 new positions on the job circuit. The steady increase in the use of personal computers will create a greater and greater demand for persons who have expertise in designing, developing, and building software for the computers.

Specialists in the fields of networks, communications, and database technologies will be in high demand across the boards as well.

There will also be a greater demand for people who can work in areas such as systems analysis, image processing, applications programming, expert systems, systems integration, multimedia programming, computer security systems, network consulting, network managing, network systems integration, and client-server designing. Who will be hiring these people? You can expect to find job opportunities working for corporations such as insurance companies, banks, and financial service companies, to name just a few of the places that will be hiring. You can expect to be able to find a job just about wherever you live. From Detroit, Michigan, to North Carolina's Research Triangle (Raleigh, Durham, and Chapel Hill), to cities in Ohio, to Silicon Valley, positions for hardware and software engineers, network specialists, PC support, database specialists, and many others are opening up at quite a rapid pace. It really makes little difference where you live. The job opportunities in the field of information technology are abundant almost everywhere. And the job opportunities for information technology specialists are expected to continue to grow, especially in the area of entry-level employment, as the pace at which computers are growing is so rapid.

The competition among companies looking to hire entry-level employees in the near future will grow fierce as the number of qualified applicants may not keep up with the demand for them. What this means for you is that if you have the skills, the education, and the knowledge to fill any of these positions, you will be in an enviable position as you will most likely be able to pick and choose your job. You will be able to pick the job that you like best, at the office that appeals the most to you, with the annual salary and benefits package that you find the most attractive. Your starting annual salary may be higher than previously expected. You may eventually find yourself in the field of education as well. This is because as the demand for information technology specialists grows, more and more young people will be seeking education in the field. Someone has to teach this ever-growing group of students, so the teaching jobs will be available to you as well. In other words, there will be more and more demand for instructors, teachers, and professors to teach in this field.

In the end, the career choice is your own. Use your judgment. Evaluate your strengths and weaknesses. Gather information. Acquire skills, knowledge, and experience. Prepare yourself, not only for your career but also for the interviews that will lead you to the job of your choice. Follow your heart and do what is right for you. It is your life and your career, and what a brilliant career it will be if you choose to pursue information technology.

Glossary

artificial intelligence   The idea of computers "knowing" how to do things and figuring things out that have previously been possible only by human beings.

chief information officer (CIO)   Person in charge of all information functions within a company.

coding writing   Detailed sets of computer instructions that follow specific needs prescribed by a systems analyst.

communications   A field that involves anything that allows two or more people to correspond and share information, in this case dealing with data and computer software and hardware.

computer architecture   The way computer circuits are structured.

database   A set of related data that is used by computer programmers and systems analysts to produce information that a particular company needs in order to run properly.

electronic network   Pathway that connects a company's computer terminals to a larger main computer.

independent contractor A person who is in business for himself or herself doing work contracted by other companies.

information science A term used interchangeably with information technology.

information technology A career field in which people take information in the form of statistics or data, process it, and then turn it into information other people can use.

Internet The international computer network that allows people around the world to communicate with one another, as well as access information through a system of Web sites.

Intranet A system similar to the Internet but that can be accessed only by people within a certain system, for example, a company.

local area network (LAN) A small network based within a company or an office building.

technical software Term for computer instructions.

wide area network (WAN) A large network that reaches a large geographical area. The Internet is considered the largest WAN.

For More Information

IN THE UNITED STATES
American Society for Information Science
8720 Georgia Avenue, Suite 501
Silver Spring, MD 20910-3602
(301) 495-0900
e-mail: asis@asis.org
Web site: http://www.asis.org

Association for Information and Image Management
1100 Wayne Avenue, Suite 1100
Silver Spring, MD 20910-5603
(301) 495-0900
(888) 839-3165
Web site: http://www.aiim.org

Association for Information Technology Professionals
315 Northwest Highway
Park Ridge, IL 60068
(847) 825-8124

Division of Information and Intelligent Systems
4201 Wilson Boulevard, Room 1115
Arlington, VA 22230
(703) 306-1930
Web site: http://www.cise.nsf.gov/iis/index.html

Information Technology Association of America
1616 N. Fort Myer Drive, Suite 1300
Arlington, VA 22209
(703) 522-5055

Society for Information Management
401 N. Michigan Avenue
Chicago, IL 60611-4267
(312) 527-6734
Web site: http://simnet.org

Software and Information Industry Association
1730 M Street NW
Washington, DC 20036-4510
(202) 452-1600
Web site: http://www.siia.net

IN CANADA
Information Technology Association of Canada
360 Albert Street, Suite 1000
Ottawa, ON K1R 7X7
(613) 238-4822
e-mail: info@itac.ca
Web site: http://www.itac.ca

For Further Reading

Applegate, Lynda M., F. Warren McFarlan, and James
    L. McKenney. *Corporate Information Science*
    Management: Text and Cases. New York: Irwin
    Professional Publishers, 1999.
Goldberg, Jan. *Great Jobs for Computer Science Majors.*
    Lincolnwood, IL: VGM Career Horizons, 1998.
Laudon, Kenneth C., and Jane Price Laudon.
    Essentials of Management Information Science.
    Engelwood Cliffs, NJ: Prentice Hall, 1998.
Stair, Lila B. *Careers in Business.* Lincolnwood, IL:
    VGM Career Horizons, 1998.
————. *Careers in Computers.* Lincolnwood, IL: VGM
    Career Horizons, 1997.

PERIODICALS
Client Server News
Communications Technology
Data Base Management
Data Communications
Datamation
Information Systems
Information Systems Management
Information Today
Information Week
Multimedia Computing and Presentations

Index

E
e-mail, 3, 11, 25, 74, 93
experience, 6, 14, 15, 26,
	29, 37, 40, 42, 43,
	45, 47, 52, 58, 68,
	72, 90, 97
expert systems, 19–20, 40, 96

G
graphics, 15, 26, 43, 70

H
hardware, 11, 15, 17, 31, 65,
	80, 84, 96

I
information
	technology/science,
	careers, examples of, 7–8,
		49–51, 58–88
	classes to take, 33–38,
		63, 85
	and computers, 1, 4, 5, 7, 8,
		9–10, 34, 60, 73, 76,
		81–83, 86, 89–90, 95
	definition of, 1, 7
	finding job in, 39–51
	management, 20–22, 39, 54,
		55, 67, 73, 74, 76,
		77–78, 82, 88
	salary, 18, 44, 52–57, 60,
		62–63, 65, 68–69, 71,
		72, 74, 77, 80, 82, 83,
		85–86, 87–88, 93, 97
	specialists, 58–88
	women and, 52–53, 71,
		90, 93

Internet, 1, 3, 12, 22–24, 27,
	28, 34, 35, 36, 42, 43,
	45–46, 58–59, 66–67,
	69, 74, 78, 80, 90, 93
	researcher, 24
Intranet, 22–24, 65

L
LAN (local area network), 12,
	25–26, 44, 77
librarian, 2, 19
library, 1, 10, 68

M
management, 18, 20–22, 24,
	26, 30, 31, 32, 39, 41,
	55, 63, 65, 67, 73, 74

N
network, 4, 7, 10, 11, 23,
	24–26, 29, 40, 44,
	58–59, 62, 74, 77,
	79–80, 85, 95, 96
	administrator, 12
	analyst, 12, 43
	definition of, 25
	engineer, 12
	manager, 12, 22, 55

O
operating systems, 14, 15, 22,
	43, 81
	definition of, 15
operations, 26

P
programming, 11, 12–16, 17,

DATE DUE

NOV 2 2001			